LONDON'S
SIGHTSEEING
BUSES

MALCOLM BATTEN

AMBERLEY

First published 2018

Amberley Publishing
The Hill, Stroud
Gloucestershire, GL5 4EP

www.amberley-books.com

Copyright © Malcolm Batten, 2018

The right of Malcolm Batten to be identified
as the Author of this work has been asserted in
accordance with the Copyrights, Designs and
Patents Act 1988.

ISBN 978 1 4456 8397 3 (print)
ISBN 978 1 4456 8398 0 (ebook)

British Library Cataloguing in Publication Data.
A catalogue record for this book is available from
the British Library.

Orgination by Amberley Publishing.
Printed in the UK.

Introduction

As the capital of the United Kingdom, and with a history going back to Roman times, London has obvious potential for tourism. As long ago as 1851 – long before London Transport had come into existence – London hosted the Great Exhibition in Hyde Park. Paxton's great Crystal Palace was later moved south of the river to the area that still bears its name, but the building burned down in 1936. In 1951 a new exhibition, entitled the Festival of Britain, was held on the South Bank of the Thames, between Waterloo Bridge and County Hall, to mark 100 years since the original. Described as 'A Tonic to the Nation' and running for six months, the Festival of Britain was a great success; a time for rejoicing after the rigours of war (although rationing was still in force). Over 8 million visitors attended this and also the Festival Pleasure Gardens at Battersea, and almost all used public transport. From 11 May four London Transport RT buses, Nos 1692, 1702, 3070 and 3114, which had toured Europe the previous year to publicise the event, inaugurated the Circular Tour of London. The fare was 2s 6d (12.5p) and the conductor used a public address system. A number of other services, worked by STL buses, provided links from stations and coach parks to the sites.

Tourism again blossomed with the coronation in 1953, but after this the tourist market was not a priority, although the sightseeing tour continued each year. In 1967 a 20-mile, two-hour-long 'London Sightseeing Round Tour' was being offered, with six journeys a day starting from Victoria. It ran from Good Friday until October at a fare of 5s (25p) for adults and half that price for children. In 1968 this became the 'Round London Sightseeing Tour' and the fare had increased to 6s (30p).

In 1970 the Round London Sightseeing Tour (RLST) carried 325,000 passengers. In 1971 the tour operated on a daily basis (except Christmas Day). From 3 April tours ran a fixed 20-mile, two-hour-long route every hour from 10.00 a.m. to 9.00 p.m., for the first time from two departure points – Piccadilly Circus and Victoria, Buckingham Palace Road. It was not pre-booked but operated on a turn-up-and-go basis and the fare was now 50p for adults and 30p for children. Services were operated by Samuelson New Transport Co. Ltd on behalf of LT.

In 1972 Britain joined the European Communities (European Union from 1993), eventually enabling visa-free travel from other member countries. It was also in 1972 that London Transport 'tested the waters' for an open-top tourist service by hiring five 1951 Park Royal-bodied Guy Arab IIIs from East Kent. East Kent provided the drivers and LT provided the conductors, while maintenance was provided by Samuelsons (soon after

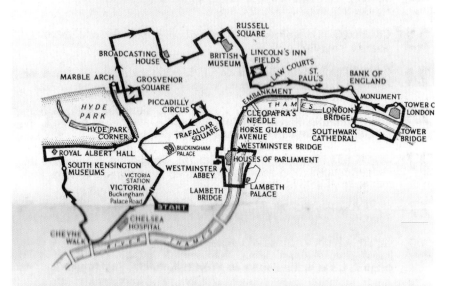

LONDON SIGHTSEEING ROUND TOUR

This two-hour circular tour of the landmarks of London covers 20 miles of the West End and City. Tours start from a point in Buckingham Palace Road between Victoria Station and Eccleston Bridge, Victoria.

The tour passes: Royal Albert Hall, Hyde Park, Marble Arch, Grosvenor Square, Law Courts, St. Paul's, Trafalgar Square, Bank of England, Monument, Tower Bridge and Tower of London. Houses of Parliament, Westminster Abbey, Piccadilly Circus. From Good Friday until October at 10 00, 11 00, 12 00, 14 00, 15 00 and 16 00.

Price 5/-, Child 2/6. Seats are not bookable.

to become one of the constituents of National Travel South East). Moreover, London Transport hired Prince Marshall (Obsolete Fleet)'s preserved former Tilling 1930 AEC Regent ST922 on a daily forty five-minute circular route (the 100) from Horse Guards Parade. This was crewed by LT and sponsored by Johnnie Walker whisky, whose adverts it carried. Both operations were obviously deemed a success, for in 1975 Obsolete Fleet supplied seven open-top former Midland Red D9s to London Transport. They were painted LT red, numbered OM1–7 and carried LT bullseye badges on their radiators. Three closed-top D9s were also provided, but these did not carry the bullseye badges. These vehicles supplemented LT's own Daimler Fleetlines, which had been used on the Round London Sightseeing Tour since 1973. In 1974, more than 600,000 passengers were carried.

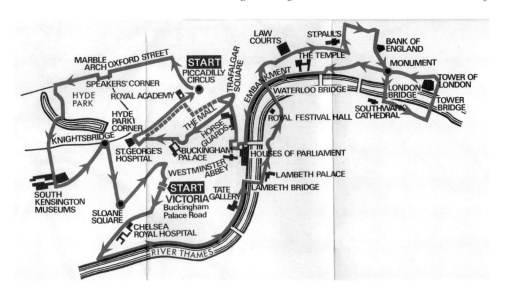

In 1978 the D9s were replaced by a batch of seven convertible Daimler Fleetlines bought by London Transport from Bournemouth Corporation, the DMO class. Both the OMs and DMOs operated out of Stockwell garage (SW).

The 1970s and early 1980s were a difficult time for bus operators, with supply problems and poor industrial relations within the manufacturing industry hindering operation. London Transport had also found that the 'off-the-shelf' vehicles they had bought since the end of Routemaster production – AEC Merlins, Swifts and Daimler Fleetlines – were less reliable than their predecessors; they even had to resort to hiring some buses from Southend Corporation at one point in 1975–6. The sightseeing tour was not top priority so vehicles were hired from a number of sources to run it, supplementing their own vehicles. The hired vehicles were painted in LT red, but some had no indication of the ownership or function other than a paper 'on hire to London Transport' notice. Among the vehicles being hired were some of the very Daimler Fleetlines that London Transport were disposing of, with Brackell, Cheam, being the first hirer, taking DMS1256. London Transport purchased twelve Routemasters from Northern General in 1979–80, who were the only other company that had bought them new. These buses, numbered RMF2761–72, might have been considered for the RLST, but in the event they were deemed as too non-standard and corroded and were sold off in 1982 without entering service.

Deregulation of coach and express services in 1980 allowed other operators to openly compete with London Transport on sightseeing services, unlike with bus routes, where LT had a monopoly until route tendering arrived in 1985. These competitors not only directly copied the pattern of tour that LT operated, they also introduced a number of new innovations, including 'hop-on, hop-off' tours and multilingual taped commentaries. Even so, by 1982 the RLST was generating some £60 million in income.

From 29 June 1984 London Regional Transport took over London Transport from the GLC. Then, from 1 April 1985, a new wholly owned subsidiary, London Buses Ltd, took on the operation of buses.

In 1986 there was a rethink on sightseeing operations. As tourists regarded the Routemaster as the iconic London bus, it was decided that these should be used on the sightseeing tour rather than the latest vehicles or hired buses. Fortunately, Routemasters were available as they were being removed from suburban routes in favour of OPO vehicles. In a £250,000 programme, fifty Routemasters were overhauled at Aldenham Works to replace the Metrobuses and hired vehicles on the RLST. They were given original style livery with a cream band and a gold, underlined fleetname. Twenty RMs were converted to open-top, while nineteen retained their roofs for use in winter or inclement weather. The other eleven buses used were RCLs, which retained their roofs and regained doors. The route was rebranded as 'The Original London Transport Sightseeing Tour' (TOLST), and adult tickets now cost £5. It was still a non-stop tour, but starting points were now at Victoria, Haymarket, Baker Street and Marble Arch. Later in the year the buses were joined by six RMAs, which had originally been used for BEA airport services, but were latterly used as staff buses to Aldenham until the works' closure.

In 1990, the versatility of the Routemaster's jig-built design would be demonstrated when ten of the RMs were lengthened by one bay to create a larger-capacity vehicle, becoming known as the ERM (extended RM) class. This was done by taking a bay from other withdrawn vehicles.

Initially the new sightseeing fleet operated out of the former Battersea garage (B), which had closed in November 1985, but from 1988 they transferred to Wandsworth garage (WD).

Also in 1986, London Buses made their first attempt at a hop-on, hop-off service with Touristlink route T2. Starting on 7 June, this was a circular route taking in most of London's tourist sites, including the Tower of London, the British Museum, Madame Tussauds, Kensington and Hyde Park. There was an all-day flat fare of £2 (£1 for children) and a short hop fare of 50p (25p for children). Metrobuses were used on this.

In preparation for eventual privatisation in the 1990s, in April 1989 London Buses was split into eleven regional operating units, plus London Coaches, who ran the sightseeing operation. When privatisation then took place, the London Coaches unit was the first to be sold in May 1992. It went to a management buyout to develop the coaching and sightseeing business. The vehicles operated out of the former Wandsworth bus garage at Jew's Row, Wandsworth, which remains their main base to date. However, the company has changed owner twice since then: in December 1997 it was bought by Arriva, and then in 2014 it was sold on to the RATP Group.

Of the many companies that joined in the competition from the 1980s, some were to be short-lived, being absorbed by other competitors, while others stayed the course to become major players. In more recent times, new companies have entered the market with varying success. Some of these have created new niche markets, such as tours of haunted London or tours with afternoon tea served en route. A mix of new and second-hand vehicles continue to provide the tours – even Routemasters can still be found on tour work.

Most of these companies over the years have offered variations on the same basic route, but nearly all passed certain key tourist attractions, such as St Paul's Cathedral and the Tower of London. Therefore, it is inevitable that many of the images shown here will be taken at these prime photographic locations.

Some other services aimed at tourists have been included here, such as special services to London Zoo and to the Thames Barrier. However, seasonal services to Wimbledon, Chelsea Flower Show and the Hampton Court Flower Show etc. are considered as outside the scope of this book. Over the years there have also been companies offering evening tours of London by night, and Christmas illuminations tours. As I never photographed any of these, they are not included. All photographs are by the author.

Flashback

RT1702 was one of four buses that inaugurated the Circular Tour of London during the Festival of Britain in 1951. It later passed into preservation. In 1976 it was posed outside the Victoria and Albert Museum, which were holding a twenty-five-year commemorative exhibition on the Festival of Britain. RT1702 was to feature again in 2000 as an exhibit in the Millennium Dome exhibition.

Early Days: London Transport/London Buses and Hired Vehicles

In 1972 London Transport 'tested the waters' for an open-top tourist service by hiring five 1951 Park Royal-bodied Guy Arab IIIs from East Kent from 17 June. FFN 378 is seen laying over in Piccadilly on 28 August. Note the tour price, which was now 65p. Tours ran from Piccadilly Circus and Victoria.

Also from 8 April 1972, London Transport hired preserved former Tilling and later General 1930 AEC Regent ST922 from Obsolete Fleet. It ran daily on circular route 100 from Horse Guards Avenue and was sponsored by Johnnie Walker whisky. Here, the bus is seen in Horse Guards Parade on 15 April 1972.

ST922 was hired again in 1973, although the routing was altered. It also ran each summer until at least 1977, in which year the route 100 ran between Trafalgar Square and the Tower of London. It is seen again at Tower Hill on 11 September 1977. Each year it ran it was sponsored by different companies, whose products it advertised; in this case, Burberrys. From 1980 to 1983 it ran hourly from the London Transport Museum in Covent Garden to Oxford Circus.

Following the apparent success of the hires from East Kent, London Transport then hired more open-top vehicles from Obsolete Fleet, the company set up by Prince Marshall. These were seven former Midland Red homemade BMMO D9 vehicles, which had passed to West Midlands PTE with local routes. Conversion to open-top was made by LPC, Hounslow. They were painted in LT red livery and given London Transport badges on their radiator grilles. OM5 approaches Chelsea Bridge on 24 August 1975.

Taking a break from tourist duties, OM4 is in Hyde Park on 10 April 1977, leading a parade of buses to launch the SRM Routemasters, which were painted in silver livery to mark the Queen's Silver Jubilee.

Other than the Obsolete Fleet OMs, London Transport used hired coaches to work the Round London Sightseeing Tour (RLST). This is a Plaxton-bodied Seddon from Capital Coaches, and was new to General, Chester-le-Street. Photographed at the Waterloo bus parking area on 5 September 1975, this site is now used as the operating base for the Red Arrow buses.

AYU 470H was a Plaxton-bodied Leyland Leopard PSU3/3RT of National Travel South East, which is painted in LT red for the RLST contract. It is seen on 30 July 1977 on the stand at Grosvenor Gardens, Victoria, which was the boarding point for the tour, with an OM in the background. AYU 469H was similarly painted for the contract and both were withdrawn in 1978.

In 1977 London Transport purchased a batch of seven Weymann-bodied convertible Daimler Fleetlines from Bournemouth Corporation. Entering service from May 1978, these became the DMO class, and DMO2 is seen loading for the Round London Sightseeing Tour at the boarding point in Grosvenor Gardens, Victoria, on 3 May 1978. Tours now ran from Marble Arch, Piccadilly and Victoria.

With the DMO class now in place, the OMs were utilised on a service to another popular tourist destination – London Zoo. The 74Z ran, as the blind indicates, between Baker Street station and the zoo, where OM7 is seen departing from the stop with a healthy load on 24 June 1978. The route ran during the Easter period and through the summer from June.

Brackell, Cheam, provided other vehicles for the sightseeing tour. This included a trio of Routemasters from Northern General, the only company outside London to purchase them. Former Northern 3103 FPT 589C was given the number RMF2761 following on from the last LT Routemaster, RML2760. It was photographed on 5 August 1978.

As well as the ex-Bournemouth Fleetlines, London Transport used some of its own latest Daimler Fleetlines on the Round London Sightseeing Tour from 1973 onwards. Devoid of any advertising, DM2631 loads at Grosvenor Gardens on 11 August 1978. These B20-type Fleetlines, with modified engine compartments to reduce noise, were allocated to the RLST from 1977.

See the sights of London from one of London's familiar sights.

Round London Sightseeing Tour

A two hour introduction to all London's principal sights.

Marble Arch, Albert Hall, the Houses of Parliament, St. Paul's, the Tower of London, Westminster Abbey and Trafalgar Square.

This 20 mile tour runs at least every hour every day from 1000-1600.

There is no guide, but take a souvenir map as you board. **Daily (except Christmas Day).**

Join the tour at Piccadilly Circus, Victoria, or Marble Arch.

Fare £1.70 (Child £1.10)

All details are subject to alteration and duration may vary with traffic conditions.

Printed in Gt. Britain © London Transport, 1979.

479/087 RP/100M

For the 1979 season, Obsolete Fleet supplied a pair of former Devon General Willowbrook-bodied AEC Regent V open-toppers for the 74Z. These retained National Bus Company red and cream livery. 507 RUO *Prince Regent* is seen at the zoo on 26 April 1979.

The other ex-Devon General AEC Regent was 508 RUO *Regency Princess*, which is seen on 14 July 1979.

On hire from Maybury, Cranborne, this former Nottingham AEC Renown with Weymann bodywork had only a paper sticker in the blind box to promote the service it was providing. It is seen at Victoria on 4 April 1980.

The following year the Obsolete Fleet Regents had received London red livery. 507 RUO is passing St Paul's Cathedral on the RLST, although it is still lettered for the zoo service. A German tourist coach is in the coach parking bay.

Passing St Paul's on 10 April 1981 is Obsolete Fleet closed-top BMMO D9 BM9 (6360 HA). Note that this does not have a London Transport roundel on its radiator grille. These three buses were withdrawn at the end of the year and were offered for sale to preservationists, although BM8 remained as a spare vehicle for the RLST in 1982. The open-top OMs remained in use into 1982.

Maybury of Cranborne, Dorset, owned this former Portsmouth Leyland Atlantean with MCW bodywork, which was hired to London Transport for the RLST. It is seen passing Victoria Library in Buckingham Palace Road on 17 April 1981. The Maybury family were to later set up London Sightseeing Tours in 1984 to compete with London Transport.

Devoid of advertising, but not at all new, Stockwell garage have put out DM1780 on the RLST on 23 April 1981. At this time the DMOs were in poor condition and were only making infrequent appearances on the service.

The unique 1966-built, rear-engined/front-entrance AEC Routemaster FRM1 last saw regular passenger work at Potters Bar garage on single-bus local route 284 until 1976. However, from 1978 until withdrawal for preservation in 1983 it put in a stint on the RLST, working from Stockwell garage. It is seen passing St Paul's on 19 September 1981. It had received an overhaul earlier in the year and a repaint into its original livery style.

London Transport regularly bought AEC buses, but had not bought the Regent V model. Obsolete Fleet DR3 (GJG 750D), a former East Kent vehicle, shows how these might have looked if they had. It shares the Victoria stand with a Daimler Fleetline on 17 April 1982.

Obsolete Fleet bought the former Northern General Routemasters from Brackell, Cheam, and continued to hire them out to London Transport. After initially working in closed-top form, they converted EUP 406B to open-top as RMT 2793. It is seen at Baker Street station on 4 September 1982 in the company of an OM on a new initiative for 1982 – a Back Street London Tour. Obsolete Fleet went into liquidation in the autumn of 1983 and so hires from them ceased.

Following the Fleetlines, London Transport bought Leyland Titans and MCW Metrobuses for its bus fleet. Titan T747 received this gold livery and the number T1983 in 1983 to mark fifty years of London Transport. It was put to work on the sightseeing tour, running from Gillingham Street garage (GM), who had taken over the tour from Stockwell in November 1982. It was photographed on 7 July 1983.

By 1983 only one of the DMO class remained operational. This was DMO3 *Stockwell Princess*, which was used to provide open-top rides at various depot open days held as part of the fifty years celebrations. Here it is seen at the Stamford Brook garage open day on 4 June. A Southend Corporation Leyland PD3 shares the duties.

London Transport continued to hire in vehicles from other companies. This Alder Valley Bristol VR is seen at Victoria on 20 June 1982. A small slipboard on the sign reads 'London Transport Coach Tours'.

London Country Bus Services comprised the former London Transport country area and Green Line operations that had been transferred to the National Bus Company in 1970. Park Royal-bodied Leyland Atlantean AN10 carries London Crusader livery as it stands outside the National Gallery on 16 October 1983 while working on the RLST. London Crusader was an NBC company set up in April 1983 to market London-based coaching activities and utilise NBC vehicles laying over in London from commuter services.

A similar vehicle, but open-topped, AN5 pauses on London Bridge with a Grey Green coach behind on 20 April 1984. The London Crusader contract (but not the vehicles) passed to Ensignbus in September 1985.

This former LT Fleetline DM1093 is from Maybury – a small sticker in the empty blind box displays the on-hire status. The side advert space has now been used to promote the service. A rival vehicle from Ebdons can be seen behind. These buses are seen on 20 April 1984.

Another company hiring vehicles back to London Transport was Ensignbus, who had the contract to dispose of the unloved Daimler Fleetlines. Former DM1682, seen on 24 May 1984, carries a pre-war-style livery, which was applied to mark fifty years of London Transport in 1983. Note the shelter for rivals Cityrama.

New London Transport Metrobuses also worked on the RLST from 1984, including M1054, seen here at Tower Hill on 25 August 1984.

With competition from other operators, London Transport decided to rebrand the RLST as 'The Official London Transport Sightseeing Tour' in 1984, as seen on M1050 on 18 August 1984. Unfortunately, some of the other operators simply pasted the word 'Official' on their vehicles too!

On hire from Holman, Crouch End, 933 GTA was one of the famous 'Sea Dog' class of convertible Leyland Atlantean buses originally used by Devon General in the Torquay area. This vehicle later also spent some time in the Limebourne Cityrama fleet. It is seen at Tower Hill on 25 August 1984.

The Thames Barrier, designed to prevent London from tidal flooding, opened in 1984. A visitor centre was provided, and London Transport was quick to realise its tourist potential. A shuttle service was provided from Greenwich, itself a popular venue for tourists, from 12 May. DM948, converted to open-top in 1983, takes on passengers when seen on 28 April 1985.

On hire from Ensignbus on 25 May 1985, early Daimler Fleetline DMO104 is now converted to open-top. It is seen at Ludgate Hill.

London Country Bus Services had provided buses on contract hire to LT for the RLST since 1982; namely, two open-top and two closed-top Atlanteans painted into LT red livery. AN108 was one such vehicle, which is seen here at London Bridge on 22 September 1985. Note that the tour now also started from Baker Street station. This is another tourist hot spot because of Madame Tussauds' waxworks and the London Planetarium.

A new innovation in 1985 was 'Touristlink'. This ran from London Zoo to the Tower of London on weekends and bank holidays using one Metrobus. M1170 departs from the Tower on 25 August 1985. A flat fare of 50p was charged. The blinds were somewhat below the standard one would normally expect from London Transport!

For 1986 the Touristlink service was revised. Touristlink route T1 was a Sunday and bank holiday service from the Tower of London to Greenwich and the Thames Barrier. Route T2 was a daily circular hop-on, hop off route around the tourist sites, starting from 7 June and worked by Metrobuses. M1172 is crossing London Bridge on this route when captured on 29 June. Passenger numbers appear to be minimal, as is any attempt at publicity on the bus.

A complete rethink of the tourist bus service took place in 1986. As tourists regarded the Routemaster as the iconic London bus, it was decided that these should be used on the sightseeing tour rather than the latest vehicles or hired buses. Fortunately, Routemasters were available as they were being removed from suburban routes in favour of OPO vehicles. The tour was renamed 'The Original London Transport Sightseeing Tour' (TOLST) and the new order is represented by RM710 at Tower Hill on 9 October 1987.

Additional Routemasters were made available by using vehicles previously in use as trainers or staff buses. RMA25 was one of the original front-entrance buses used for the BEA airport service, six of which joined the OLST fleet in 1987. It is seen at Tower Hill on the same day.

London Buses also acquired some of the former Northern General Routemasters that had previously been hired from Obsolete Fleet. RMT2793, originally Northern General 3090, looks smart in its London red livery as it crosses London Bridge on 23 August 1987. However, as their equipment was non-standard, these vehicles were not retained for long.

London Coaches

Despite the vagaries of British weather, open-top buses were preferred by tourists, so twenty Routemasters were suitably converted. RM1864 pauses on London Bridge, from where top-deck passengers can photograph Tower Bridge and HMS *Belfast*, on 18 March 1990.

The RCL class had originally been built for Green Line use. They passed to London Country in 1970 but most of the LCBS Routemasters were sold back to London Transport in the late 1970s. In 1980, forty RCLs were overhauled and modified as red buses, losing their doors and twin headlights in the process. By 1984, all of these had been taken out of service, but in 1986 eleven were transferred to the sightseeing fleet. New doors, air-operated by the driver, were fitted for winter use. RCL2259 is taking a break from its usual duties by appearing at the British Coach Rally, held at Southampton, on 29 April 1990. Note the lettering for a multi-lingual taped commentary – a feature first introduced by rival company Limebourne Cityrama.

A revised advertising style indicating some of the key locations passed was applied to vehicles such as RM242, which is seen on London Bridge on 26 May 1990. It was first applied to the ERMs (*see below*).

To increase capacity, especially as most passengers wanted to travel upstairs in sunny weather, London Coaches created the ERM (extended RM) class of ten open-top buses in 1990. Making the most of the versatility of the Routemaster design, with its front and rear sub-sections, an extra bay from withdrawn vehicles was inserted into the middle of an RM. This made them longer than an RML and increased the seating from sixty-four to seventy-six. The modifications were carried out by Kent Engineering of Canterbury. Seen on 26 May 1990, ERM 80 crosses London Bridge.

In 1990 ten of the RCLs were converted to have removable centre sections on their roofs. RCL2243 passes the Law Courts in Aldwych on 7 July 1991.

London Coaches introduced a new livery and fleet name for their vehicles. From 17 August 1991, before privatisation, they also introduced 'London Plus' – a ninety-minute, thirty-stop hop-on, hop-off tour – to compete with those offered by rival companies. The fare was £8 for two days of unlimited travel. RM704 displays the new regime at Hyde Park Corner on 23 August 1992.

In 1991 London Coaches acquired three 1984 Dennis Dominators with Northern Counties bodies that London Buses had bought for comparison trials while deciding what should succeed the Leyland Titans and MCW Metrobuses. H3 is seen rounding Aldwych on 28 August 1992. The buses did not last long, with H2 and H3 being sold on to Capital Citybus for use on tendered routes they had won.

Perhaps seen as a retrograde step, London Coaches applied overall advertising to some buses – a practice favoured by some rivals but eschewed by London Buses. RCL2235 heads up Park Lane towards Marble Arch while promoting the golden arches of McDonalds on 31 August 1992.

London Coaches were also developing a private hire business, and RCL2260 displays this aspect at the Wandsworth garage on 19 February 1994. This was the only RCL not to be open-topped – a factor that has led to its eventual preservation and return to Green Line livery.

Like Ensignbus, London Coaches bought a number of MCW Metroliner double-deck coaches that had previously been used on National Express services. Most were converted to open-top, such as this example seen in Park Lane on 6 August 1994. This had started out with Oxford as B904 XJO.

Advertising for restaurant Planet Hollywood has been applied to RCL2250, seen rounding Marble Arch on 29 March 1996. This even had Contra Vision advertising over the lower deck windows.

The Bristol VR, while being a standard bus for National Bus Company fleets, was not purchased by London Transport. However, London Coaches purchased a number of these second hand to replace the ex-BEA RMAs. Most had the standard ECW body, but a few – like former East Kent TFN 989T – had Willowbrook bodies. BW8 is seen passing St Paul's on 31 March 1996.

Seen on 13 July 199, the more familiar ECW bodywork is carried by VDV 112S, a former Devon General Bristol VR that was converted to open-top.

As with most other sightseeing operators, the London Transport Daimler Fleetline entered the fleet. This is former DM1040, seen in Whitehall on 30 March 1997. The half open-top arrangement allowed for some protection to upper-deck passengers from wind and rain.

Other Fleetlines received the full open-top treatment, such as KUC 176P, seen passing Trafalgar Square on 30 March 1997.

In 1996–7 a promotion for the Tower of London led to a number of London Coaches vehicles receiving promotional livery, as seen on Willowbrook-bodied Bristol VR TFN 988T. The bus is laying over at Hyde Park Corner on 7 July 1997.

In order to cater for disabled passengers, RM307 and RM450 had been fitted with wheelchair lifts in 1988. The double-door access for this can be seen on RM450, which is seen in overall advertising livery for Radio Medway at the Showbus Rally at Duxford Airfield on 21 September 1997.

Arriva TOLST/RATP

London Coaches' sightseeing business and vehicles were sold to Arriva in December 1997. They acquired the licences and goodwill of the Ensignbus sightseeing fleet in March 2001, trading as London Pride and City Sightseeing (qv). Since then some of the Arriva TOLST vehicles have carried the City Sightseeing livery and fleet name. On 11 September 2014 the company was bought by RATP Dev of Paris, who are also the owners of the London United and London Sovereign bus companies. The original Wandsworth garage is still used, plus an outstation at Rainham – the old London Pride site.

In 2018 there is the main Original Tour running every fifteen to twenty minutes, with twenty-five stopping points and taking approximately two and a half hours for the full circuit. This runs alternately as yellow T1 with a live guide and T2 with digitally recorded commentary in English and ten other languages. A one-hour blue T4 Royal Borough Tour serves the Kensington shopping and museums district, again with digitally recorded commentary. The orange T5 West End & British Museum Tour links Piccadilly Circus with the British Museum, which also has digitally recorded commentary. Feeder services extend to Euston and King's Cross stations until 12.00 p.m. Capital Connector routes T6 and T7 feed into Marble Arch from Kensington and Paddington (T6) or Marylebone Road/Baker Street (T7). There is a free City Cruises sightseeing river cruise pass provided with 24-hour or 48-hour tickets, and three free walking tours are also available. Free Wi-Fi is available and there is an Original Tour app.

London Coaches were bought by the Arriva Group in December 1997. This ERM, seen passing St Paul's on 27 May 1999, shows how the livery was adapted to reflect the corporate style of the parent company. Note also that the bus has lost its original registration and has been re-registered. The ten ERMs would be withdrawn in 2002 and sold to Mac Tours, Edinburgh, for further use.

By 2000 the London Bus companies were withdrawing Leyland Titans and MCW Metrobuses as new low-floor single and double-deckers were entering their fleets. Some of these were snapped up by the sightseeing companies. London Coaches started to buy in Metrobuses and Arriva transferred further examples from their own London bus fleets. M748 came from Arriva London North (formerly Leaside) and was at Hyde Park Corner on 12 March 2000.

In 2002, to celebrate the Queen's Golden Jubilee, Arriva TOLST painted former M555 in this version of their national blue and cream livery. It is seen at Victoria on 14 June.

VVN 203Y, a Dennis Dominator with Northern Counties bodywork, was new to Cleveland Transit. Note the lettering for City Sightseeing London and the offside door that has been fitted. It is seen at Victoria on 9 June 2003.

To provide high capacity and replace the MCW Metroliners, MCW Metrobus three-axle vehicles were sourced from New World First Bus, Hong Kong, from 2001. EMB 764 is seen at Baker Street station on 19 June 2005. These vehicles could carry seventy-five passengers on the upper deck.

The first new vehicles to enter the Arriva TOLST fleet were these stylish Volvo B7L vehicles with open-top bodywork, which were built by the Spanish company Ayats. VLY904 pulls away from the stop in Buckingham Palace Road outside Victoria station on 12 July 2005. Four similar vehicles were bought by Ensignbus for their provincial City Sightseeing ventures.

Cascaded from the Arriva London bus feet were these Alexander-bodied Volvo Olympians. J324 BSH carries City Sightseeing London livery, as is now carried by several vehicles in the fleet. It was photographed at St Paul's Cathedral on 11 June 2006.

The first low-floor double-deckers to be cascaded included DLP213, a Plaxton-bodied DAF. Again, it is seen at St Paul's on 11 June 2006.

As regulations on accessibility and emissions levels began to become significant, Arriva TOLST invested in more new vehicles. A batch of Volvo B9TLs with East Lancs Visionaire bodywork came in 2007. VLE616 prepares to turn into the Victoria coach station extension in Bulleid Way, over Victoria station, on 11 September 2007.

The VLE class were followed by a three-axle version, giving greater capacity. VXE726 is seen at the same location on 26 March 2012.

One of the smart Ayats-bodied VLY class is viewed again, this time carrying the City Sightseeing livery at Victoria in 2014.

In 2014 TOLST was sold from Arriva to the RATP Group, who also owned London United. Looking much the same, except for the RATP Group lettering on the front and over the driver's window, DLP259 lays over on the Embankment near Hungerford Bridge.

New vehicles received in 2016–17 were Ayats Bravo open-toppers. One of them, YXY792, has just turned into Park Lane by Marble Arch on 6 April 2017.

In 2017 a new livery based on the Union Jack was introduced. This was applied to both new and earlier vehicles in the fleet. Representing the new order is DLP248, seen passing Grosvenor Gardens, Victoria, on 10 July. Just passing the other way is a 'New Routemaster' of Go-Ahead London General in a pre-war commemorative livery.

A revised version of the City Sightseeing livery was applied in 2018. VLE615 displays this as it heads up Park Lane on 15 May.

Other Sightseeing Companies

London Cityrama

Although operating on sightseeing tours since at least 1975, London Cityrama was established as a separate entity from its parent company, Limebourne, in July 1982. The company was sold to Ensignbus on 8 November 1993 and was absorbed into the latter's London Pride operation.

One of the earliest competing companies was London Cityrama. An early acquisition was 302 TR, a Leyland PD2 with a somewhat ungainly Park Royal body that had started life with Southampton City Transport. On 5 April 1975 it was at Grosvenor Gardens, Victoria, in an advertising livery.

By 1976, 302 TR was in fleet livery. London Cityrama pioneered the use of taped commentaries in various languages and the bus advertises this facility. The languages offered were English, French, German, Italian, Spanish, Dutch, Swedish and Japanese. Britain had joined the EEC by then, so European tourists might be expected, but it is interesting to see that Japanese tourists were significant that far back. 302 TR is seen here on 19 April 1976.

Cityrama LLH 6K was a Roe-bodied Leyland Atlantean that had originally been purchased new by Halls Silverline, Hounslow. It was on the Victoria stand on 17 April 1981. This bus was later converted to open-top and passed to Culture Bus.

JWF 47W was another Roe-bodied Atlantean, but this was bought new by Cityrama in 1981. It is seen on 30 May 1982 at the former coach park by Gloucester Road station. This location closed after it was deemed that it was in use as a coach station without planning permission.

On hire to Cityrama on 20 April 1984 is Southend Corporation open-top Daimler Fleetline WJN 372J, which has Northern Counties bodywork. It is seen pulling away from Grosvenor Gardens, Victoria – the starting point for many tour operators. Vehicles from competing companies can be seen on the stand.

Passing St Paul's on 30 May 1985, XWX 388G is a 1969 Bristol VR with an ECW body, and has been converted to open-top. It started life with West Yorkshire.

Cityrama were one of a number of the sightseeing companies who chose to accept overall advertising on some of their buses. RCH 515F was an ex-Trent Leyland Atlantean that carried advertising for Thai Airline. This was the first version of the livery and was photographed on 6 August 1988 in Grosvenor Place, Victoria.

By 24 July 1990, when this picture was taken, RCH 515F was carrying an amended version of the Thai Airlines livery. A number of ex-LT Fleetlines carried a similar livery.

Most of the companies who competed for the sightseeing trade bought former London Transport Daimler Fleetlines when LT chose to withdrawn them after a short life. Cityrama were no exception and OUC 36R was formerly DM2036. It is seen standing outside the entrance to the National Gallery in Trafalgar Square on 19 February 1989. This side of the square was later pedestrianised under Ken Livingston's term as Mayor of London.

This imaginative livery for BP was carried by Fleetline KJD 104P on 12 November 1988. At least the solution suggested would be a zero-emissions bus!

Superior comfort and views are afforded by this Jonckheere-bodied Scania coach, which is seen conveying tourists across London Bridge on 27 March 1989.

Optare-bodied Leyland Olympian E964 PME in Aldwych. This is one of two buses that were surplus to an order from Boro'line Maidstone and bought by Cityrama in 1988 for tendered bus operations. When the contracts ended, the buses were transferred to sightseeing work and open-topped. It is seen here on 7 July 1991.

Destination London

Destination London were the owners of this Bristol VRLLH6L with ECW bodywork, which was originally with the Standerwick fleet of Ribble Motor Services. It was at Victoria on 2 May 1977 when seen. A similar vehicle, LRN 56J, was painted in LT red livery and ran on hire to London Transport.

Guards, London/Vintage Bus Company

Guards of London W1, trading as the Vintage Bus Company, operated this vehicle, which ran a tour on behalf of Hanover Grand Hotels. It was one of three former Leicester Corporation Leyland PD3/1s, which had been rebuilt to look like pre-war vehicles with open rear staircases. It was passing St Paul's Cathedral on 4 April 1980 when seen. Some ex-London RTs – RT2461, RT4599 and RT4613 – were also similarly 'aged', as was an ex-Maynes of Manchester AEC Regent V, 6972 ND.

Culture Bus

One problem with the Round London Sightseeing Tour and Cityrama's Tours were that they were non-stop tours; thus, tourists could not alight to visit the attractions passed en route. Some American cities and Sydney, Australia, did offer tours wherein one could disembark at will and reboard a later tour. Two Australian women visiting Britain in 1980 noticed this situation and approached Mike Doyle, the manager of Wealden Coaches, Twickenham, to see if such a service could be started in London. They formed Culture Bus Ltd and put in application for a licence in April 1981. This was refused by London Transport on the grounds of abstracting passengers and increasing traffic congestion. However, an appeal was made to the Metropolitan Traffic Commissioners in March 1982, for which detailed costings were prepared with the experience of some directors of Cityrama, who joined Culture Bus. This time they were successful, subject to agreeing stopping places with the Metropolitan Police, and final approval was given in March 1983. Services commenced on 17 May 1983.

Five Leyland-engined DMS Fleetlines were acquired via Ensignbus and four were needed to operate the thirty-minute frequency tours. No commentary was given but public address was fitted for the driver to announce stops and nearby attractions. Fares at the commencement of service were: £2.50 for adults, £1.50 for children and £7 for a family ticket. Tickets purchased after 3.00 p.m. were valid for the next day too.

Culture Bus later came under the ownership of Trathens, Plymouth, but was put up for sale when Trathens went into liquidation in 1985. They were then bought out by Ensignbus from 30 September 1985.

The Culture Bus service offered twenty stops with all-day travel. Fleetlines were used, such as former DM2000, seen here at Hyde Park Corner on 28 April 1985.

Uniquely among the tour operators, Culture Bus bought some Scania Metropolitan double-deckers. Former London Transport MD6 is at Hyde Park Corner on 21 July 1985. Note the lettering for attractions en route.

Harrods

From 26 August 1983 patrons of high-class store Harrods could enjoy a sightseeing tour of London. It was not a clapped-out ex-London Fleetline that was provided for them; no, they travelled in one of two luxury 1983 Neoplan N122 coaches owned by Eurocare Travel, Isleworth. The fare was initially £10 and included refreshments served by a hostess. A122 RTL is seen on London Bridge on 22 September 1985.

London Sightseeing Tours

London Sightseeing Tours was set up by the Maybury family in 1984. Previously, they had been hiring out vehicles to London Transport. The business and vehicles were bought by Ensignbus in 1995 and were added to their London Pride operations.

A former Portsmouth Leyland Atlantean contrasts with ex-LT Fleetline DMS141 as they stand in the yard at Battersea on 21 May 1985.

Crossing London Bridge on 29 January 1989 is TOE 463N, an East Lancs-bodied Daimler Fleetline, which was formerly known as West Midlands 4463.

Former London Fleetline KUC 982P was treated to this attractive livery, which gave prospective punters a map showing some of the attractions that would be seen en route. It was awaiting custom outside the National Gallery, Trafalgar Square, when seen on 9 April 1989.

Fleetline KUC 944P was given an overall advert to promote Tobacco Dock. This Grade I listed former dockyard site in Wapping, east of Tower Bridge, had been redeveloped in 1990 as a shopping, dining and entertainment centre to rival Covent Garden. Some of the tourist bus routes started to include it in their itinerary. Unfortunately, it failed to live up to expectations and closed soon after. Part of the site is now used for filming and corporate events. KUC 944P is seen on 18 March 1990.

The most unusual vehicle operated by London Sightseeing Tours was this 1958 Leyland PD2 with Park Royal bodywork, which was rebuilt in the 'vintage' style with an open rear staircase. Re-registered as LST 873, it had started out as Barrow Corporation CEO 952. On 31 August 1992 it was passing the Merchant Seaman's war memorial on Tower Hill when caught on film.

Another Leyland in the fleet was this smart former Southdown 'Queen Mary' PD3 with a Northern Counties full-front body. Re-registered as BHM 288, the bus is seen at Ludgate Hill on 3 April 1994. It had previously been with Kings Ferry, Gillingham, with whom it carried the registration PRX 207B. The original Southdown registration was 410 DCD.

London Sightseeing Tours ran a hop-on, hop-off service, which was mainly worked by both closed and open-top ex-London Fleetlines in a white livery. Some vehicles also had an offside doorway added, as on KJD 82P, which is seen passing St Paul's on 8 April 1994. This was for loading at the offside kerb in Lower Regent Street.

London Sightseeing Tours also acquired some of the long-lived Leyland PD3 open-toppers that were new to Brighton Corporation, but latterly operated with Wightline on the Isle of Wight. Former Brighton 34 is proceeding down Whitehall on 18 February 1995.

Ebdon's Tours

Coach operator Ebdon's of Sidcup joined the competition in 1984. However, their sightseeing operations were sold to Ensignbus in December 1985.

Their most interesting vehicle was to be the oldest bus used on sightseeing duties, other than the preserved ST922 of Prince Marshall. Dating from 1949, KTF 591 was a Park Royal-bodied AEC Regent III that had started out as Morecambe & Heysham Corporation 62. It then became Lancaster 591 when the fleets merged. It is seen at London Transport's shelter at Victoria on 20 April 1984, with a Cityrama bus behind. The competition was hotting up!

By 25 August 1984, when KTF 591 was photographed again at Tower Hill, the lettering had been amended. Note the addition of the word 'Official' – after London Transport rebranded their tour as 'The Official London Transport Sightseeing Tour', although other companies plastered the word on their vehicles.

Most of Ebdon's buses were ex-London Fleetlines. One innovation they introduced was the 'Photobus', which involved removing the upper-deck windows on some vehicles while retaining the roof. KUC 138P illustrates this practice as it passes St Paul's on 18 September 1984.

By contrast, former DMS158 is in largely unmodified condition when seen at Victoria on 26 April 1985.

London Pride

London Pride was founded in March 1984 with ex-London Transport Fleetlines. In March 1985 the company was taken over by Ensignbus, who formed a new company, London Pride Sightseeing Ltd, to take over the operations.

London Pride started operations using the customary ex-London Transport Fleetlines. They were taken over by Ensignbus, who retained the fleet name for their own operations. MLK 648L is at Tower Hill on 25 August 1984.

London Tour Co.

In the 1980s, London Tour Co. were another company who tried their luck in the London sightseeing market. They were acquired by Ensignbus (London Pride) in 1990.

The customary ex-LT Fleetlines, such as GHV 110N, made their presence known. Their departure point was in Coventry Street, Piccadilly, but they followed the usual route, and so the bus is seen crossing London Bridge, southbound, on 29 June 1986.

On a somewhat gloomier 12 October 1986, an ex-South Yorkshire PTE Alexander-bodied Leyland Atlantean, SWB 286L, has only a handful of passengers.

On 23 August 1987, it is the turn of a somewhat elderly 1965 Leyland Atlantean, which started life with the Salford City Transport fleet, until that undertaking became part of Greater Manchester PTE.

On 28 January 1990, this early Bristol VR is seen at Tower Hill. I always felt that this company's vehicles came across as rather scruffier and less professionally presented than their competitors. Perhaps this is why they didn't last long.

Ensignbus

In 1985 dealers Ensignbus moved into competition on the sightseeing services rather than just hiring vehicles to London Transport. From 1986 they were also running tendered bus services. A blue and silver livery was adopted for both operations. In March 1985 they took over London Pride, and in October they formed a new company, London Pride Sightseeing Ltd. Following the liquidation of owning company Trathens, from 30 September 1985 they took over Culture Bus. From the same date they gained the contract for London Crusader sightseeing work. This was followed by the takeover of the sightseeing operations of Ebdon's of Sidcup in December 1985. By now they claimed to be London's largest sightseeing operator, but they resisted the temptation to move upmarket, with Managing Director Leon Daniels saying: 'We dug our heels in and unashamedly sold a Southend seafront-type service in central London with old open-top buses.'

With an operating base at Purfleet, there was a lot of dead mileage, which they tried to offset by running morning and evening commuter journeys. These were not compatible, however: tourists wanted open-toppers, but commuters didn't, so this ended in 1987. The Culture Bus name was not retained and this part of the business was sold to Southend Transport from April 1987. London Tour Co. was acquired in 1990, followed by London Sightseeing Tours in 1995. In 1995 they introduced the first LPG-powered bus to London when they converted one of their MCW Metroliners as diesel emissions were becoming an environmental issue.

In 1999 Ensignbus launched the City Sightseeing global franchise brand, starting with an operation in Seville. This quickly grew and in May 2002 Ensign would acquire the assets of Guide Friday, who ran open-top tours in many British towns and cities (but not London), and these vehicles would adopt the City Sightseeing brand and livery.

Ensignbus sold their London sightseeing licences and goodwill to Arriva TOLST in March 2001. Thereafter, some TOLST vehicles have carried City Sightseeing livery.

As Ensignbus had the contract to dispose of LT's Daimler Fleetlines, it was inevitable that these would be used on both sightseeing and tendered bus services. JGF 343K is at Tower Hill on 6 October 1985. This and DMS33 were used to operate the 1985/6 winter season tours on behalf of London Crusader.

Ensignbus bought out Culture Bus in 1985 and former DM2000 is seen again under new ownership at Tower Hill on 3 November 1985. The name was not retained, Ensignbus choosing to use the London Pride name instead, which they had also bought out.

Many of the Ensignbus Fleetlines carried overall advertising liveries over the next few years. Probably the most extreme was that carried by MLK 586L for an Aussie beer. It was travelling down the Strand on 13 August 1989 when photographed.

It wasn't just ex-LT Fleetlines, other vehicles were pressed into service from dealer stock, such as this ex-Ribble Leyland Atlantean, seen on 25 June 1989. It was originally Blackburn Corporation 94.

The first vehicles bought new by Ensignbus for their London Pride operations were four Leyland Olympians with Northern Counties bodywork. One such was G132 YWC, seen here on 18 November 1989. Note the PT (Purfleet) garage code, London style, and the 'Official' lettering and 'rubber stamp' motif copied from that formerly used by London Buses on the RLST.

Larger capacity vehicles were sourced in the form of MCW Metroliner coaches from 1990. Seen converted to open-top and with sixty-seven seats upstairs on 6 July 1991, former Shamrock & Rambler A113 KFX at Tower Hill shows the red and silver livery and London Pride fleet name adopted for the sightseeing operation. Vehicles on bus work retained blue and silver.

In 1994 Ensignbus introduced a tour that went to 'Docklands and Greenwich'. The Canary Wharf area on the Isle of Dogs was being redeveloped as a major financial district at this time. Greenwich was already a major tourist centre of attraction, but to reach it bus tourists would need to walk through the pedestrian tunnel from Island Gardens as there was no road bridge, and the Docklands Light Railway would not be extended under the river to Lewisham until 1999. Fleetline KJD 91P is seen at Tower Hill on 2 April 1994.

Ensignbus had begun to accumulate a number of heritage vehicles. RT3232 was painted in the sightseeing livery and was working on this service on the same day. In this view it has just departed from Tower Hill. RT3062 was similarly painted; both had previously been used on the Culture Bus service in blue/silver livery in January and February 1986 – a quieter season when their limited capacity was less of a problem.

Returning from a Docklands and Greenwich tour on the same day is UJF 182, an ex-Leicester Corporation 1959 Daimler CS6G/30 with Metro-Cammell bodywork, which had come via Cityrama (who had used it as a trainer). Before this it had been with well-known Durham independents OK of Bishop Auckland and then Lockey of West Auckland.

Crossing London Bridge on 22 July 1995 is this former Nottingham vehicle. It is in the livery of Guide Friday, who had been previously running it in York. This company operated sightseeing tours in a number of other towns and cities, but not in London, although they had put in an unsuccessful bid for London Coaches when it was first privatised. It was on hire to Ensignbus at the time, so it shows what might have been if the bid had been successful. Meanwhile, Ensignbus Metroliner B117 ORU was being converted to LNG by Guide Friday.

Ensignbus took over London Sightseeing Tours in April 1995. Ex-Brighton Leyland PD3 MCD 134F is seen again, now with London Pride lettering, at Tower Hill on 31 March 1996. Along with other operators, Ensignbus posted vehicles at prime boarding points. Passengers could obtain information and tickets here and wait on the stationary bus until the next tour bus came along.

Another of the ex-Brighton vehicles is seen in Prince Albert Road, Marylebone, on 5 April 1996. A new series of numbered routes were introduced from 30 March, with route 1 running from London Zoo to Tower of London, route 2 linking the Kensington museums with the British Museum, and route 4 running as the Tower to Docklands service.

Transferred from the heritage fleet for sightseeing work in 1996 was ex-London Transport RT4169, which had been converted to open-top. It was noted in Russell Square on 6 May 1996. Over 100 buses were diagrammed to work the peak summer programme.

Ensignbus acquired Limebourne Cityrama in 1993 and with them came the taped commentary tours. This ex-LT MCW Metrobus carries the London Pride name but also the Cityrama name on the blind and flags to indicate the languages available. A red and gold variant livery was also applied. It is seen on London Bridge on 28 March 1997.

Ensignbus introduced more numbered routes, which began picking up at some new locations. This former Eastbourne Dennis Dominator is seen outside the Great Northern Hotel at King's Cross while working route 7 on 5 June 1999.

On route 8, this former Cleveland Transit Dennis Dominator displays a variant livery style and an offside door at Victoria station on 12 March 2000.

Ensignbus sold their sightseeing business to Arriva TOLST in March 2001. However, on 20 July 2013 pre-war RT8 from their heritage fleet was recorded rounding Marble Arch while working 'The Wartime London Tour' on behalf of www.wartimelondon.com.

Blue Triangle

Blue Triangle entered the market in 1985. Their sightseeing operations were sold to London Coaches on 15 March 1997, with nine open-top DMS Fleetlines passing over with the sale. Their other operations continued, including rail replacement services and tendered bus services in Essex, and later in London from 1999.

Former Northern General Routemaster FPT 588C had already seen the rounds on the sightseeing circuit with Brackell and Obsolete Fleet when it was acquired in January 1987. It seems to be carrying a full upstairs load as it crosses London Bridge on 23 August 1987.

FJY 918E was a MCW-bodied Leyland Atlantean that had originated with Plymouth Corporation. This was also in use on 23 August 1987.

The bulk of the fleet consisted of the ubiquitous ex-London Transport Daimler Fleetlines. Open-top Fleetline JGF 404K passes St Paul's on 28 August 1994.

London Country Bus Services

In 1986 the four Atlanteans that had operated for London Transport in London Crusader livery – ANs 5, 10, 106, and 110 – were repainted to work the Green Line Round London Sightseeing Tour. This tour ran hourly from 8 June, starting from Trafalgar Square. Vehicles operated from the National London Catford garage. From 7 September 1986 London Country was split into four separate companies and these vehicles passed to London Country South East. They changed their name to Kentish Bus in 1987.

London Country AN5 is seen again on London Bridge in July 1986, but now in this Green Line livery.

Southend Transport

Like Ensignbus, Southend Transport had built up a large commuter operation to London. In fact, by 1986 over sixty coaches were in use. The problem was what to do with them between the peak hours. Southend bought the Culture Bus brand from Ensignbus on 1 April 1987. As single-deck coaches were not ideal for tourists, Southend hired six coach-seated buses from Cardiff, but the service wasn't marketed on the ground effectively and lost money. Moreover, commuter traffic was declining because of traffic congestion and aggressive marketing by Network SouthEast to get passengers back on trains. The operation was reduced to hourly in November and ended on 19 December 1987.

Ensignbus did not keep the Culture Bus brand, selling this on to Southend Transport. Southend used these East Lancs-bodied coach-seated Leyland Olympians on long-term hire from Cardiff Corporation. B554 ATX passes St Paul's on 17 April 1987.

Big Bus Company

Big Bus Company was started by members of the Maybury family in 1991. They had previously been associated with London Sightseeing Tours. They started with two vehicles. From 26 March 1994 they joined the ranks of companies offering a hop-on, hop-off service with their Stopper Tour. From 1 April this ran every fifteen minutes, with fourteen stops and a London Tourist Board guide giving a commentary. A 24-hour ticket cost £12 for adults. By 1996 they claimed to have 25 per cent of the market. A new initiative for 1996 was a tie-in with London United's Airbus, wherein tourists staying at hotels near Heathrow could get a return ticket to Central London on the Airbus service and a sightseeing tour for a combined price of £20 for adults.

In 2018 they provide a main Red Route hop-on, hop-off circular tour with fourteen stops running every ten to twenty minutes and live commentary in English. A longer Blue Route circular tour includes Baker Street, Paddington station and the Kensington area. This has the same frequency but has a recorded commentary in twelve languages. The Green Route links Charing Cross with Euston and King's Cross stations via the British Museum. This runs every twenty to thirty minutes and has recorded commentary. River cruises and walking tours are included in the tickets, which are for one, two or three days. There is free Wi-Fi and a Big Bus app.

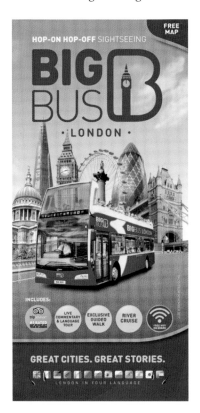

Their flagship vehicle became PFN 853, a 1959 AEC Regent V with a full-front Park Royal body that had been converted to open-top by its original owners, East Kent, for seaside work in the Margate area. Bought from preservation, the East Kent livery was adopted for the fleet and its image was included in the company logo. Here it is seen passing the Law Courts in the Strand on 7 July 1991.

The much-travelled Routemaster FPT 588C came to Big Bus from Blue Triangle in April 1992, and how magnificent it looked in its new colours! Two other ex-Northern General Routemasters were acquired from preservationists – FPT 592C and FPT 603C – both of which retained their roofs. Big Bus kept their vehicles in superb condition, whatever their age, and it is perhaps no surprise that they have stayed the course right up to 2018 while others have fallen by the wayside.

Another elderly vehicle entering the fleet in 1991 was this Metro-Cammell-bodied Leyland PD2/12. Now re-registered XMD 47A, it had started out with Trent while registered KCH 106. It had later been used in open-top form by Grey Green. By 3 November 1993, when photographed at Hyde Park Corner, it was being used as a static boarding-point promotional bus.

Former Greater Manchester Leyland Atlantean LJA 603P enters Parliament Square on 4 May 1992. Note the reference to a live commentary, as compared to the taped commentaries offered by some rivals.

Like most of the other operators, Big Bus took some London Fleetlines – but in their case they looked smarter than when new to LT. One of the later B20 models, THX 328S, with a modified engine bustle, is seen at Tower Hill on 31 August 1992.

A Routemaster, originally registered RM272 (VLT 272), passes St Paul's on 12 October 1997.

Big Bus bought London Buses' Leyland Titans when they started to become available. Former T1056 has been converted to open-top but with a retractable tarpaulin roof for use in inclement weather. It is also lettered for their version of a taped language tour, with twelve different languages on offer. Note the logo with a headphone and the Regent V emblem. It is seen here on 2 April 1999.

Like Arriva TOLST, Big Bus turned to Hong Kong for a source of larger-capacity vehicles. Three-axle MCW Metrobus vehicles were bought, such as this, seen here passing St Paul's on 15 June 2002. These could seat sixty-one passengers on the upper deck. Note the registration – B16 BSS ('Big Bus' – get it?).

Also bought were Dennis Condor three-axle vehicles such as this one, seen in Piccadilly at Green Park on 28 July 2004. Some were full open-top while others were converted, with just the rear portion being open.

With the requirement to provide accessible vehicles, Big Bus bought twelve of these 2001–2-built Dennis Tridents with East Lancs bodies from Metrobus. In half open-top form, LV51 YCH proceeds along Whitehall on 16 February 2008.

When Big Bus bought their first new buses in 2008, they selected Volvo B9TLs with East Lancs or Optare Visionaire bodywork. DA211 is a 2009 delivery, seen here in Whitehall on 19 April 2009.

Like Arriva TOLST, they followed these up with a three-axle equivalent. DA326 passes St Paul's on 24 April 2011.

A revised livery style was introduced, as seen on DA203 at Baker Street station on 27 May 2013. This removed the logo featuring the East Kent Regent V – a vehicle that had long since departed the fleet – and replaced it with an image of Big Ben.

It was the next batch of new vehicles in 2012 that was to make the greatest news in the long story of London's sightseeing buses, for these were sourced new from China. They were Anhui Ankai HFF612 models and seated fifty-seven upstairs and twenty-five downstairs. AN343 heads along Whitehall on 2 June 2013.

In 2016 this Plaxton-bodied Volvo was given this promotional livery for use as a static sales/enquiry bus. On 24 September it was at their pitch outside Charing Cross station.

The latest vehicles to enter the fleet are Dennis Tridents with Alexander Enviro 400 bodies that were previously with Abelio London. DA223, passing St Paul's on 14 May 2017, is followed by a similarly bodied bus of Tower Transit.

London Northern

In 1993 a special commercial service to London Zoo was revived by London Northern, one of the separate operating fleets of London Buses that had been created in 1989, in readiness for later privatisation. The route was numbered Z1.

One vehicle used was this open-top Fleetline D2556, photographed on 13 August.

The other vehicle in use on this occasion was open-top Metrobus M804. Note the lack of passengers on either vehicle.

In 1994 London Northern was privatised, along with the other London Buses companies. In 1995 M804 received this new Sightseers livery for the route, which it was photographed using on 22 July 1995. D2556 was also used, but was in overall red with the Sightseers name.

Frog Tours/Duck Tours

In 2000 a new variation on the tourist service was created when Frog Tours started their business. Using nine converted former American amphibious DUKW military vehicles, Frog Tours combined a sightseeing tour on London's streets with a trip along the River Thames. Tours departed from the south bank of the river near County Hall. The company was later renamed (perhaps more appropriately) Duck Tours.

In 2013 the buoyancy foam in one DUKW caught fire while on the Thames, causing services to be suspended until remedial treatment was made. London Duck Tours ceased trading in September 2017 because of the loss of the ramp that they used to access the Thames near Vauxhall Bridge, this site being required for the construction of the Thames Water super sewer.

Cleopatra, one of their vehicles (vessels?) is seen in the river near Westminster Bridge on 19 July 2001.

Seen here on dry land, *Titania* heads down Grosvenor Place, Victoria, on 5 September 2004, with a Routemaster on route 73 behind. Buckingham Palace is behind the wall.

Heritage Routemaster Routes

The London Routemaster bus, first entering regular service in 1959, was to have a much longer life than originally envisaged and achieved iconic status. Although withdrawals started in the mid-1980s, they were retained on central London trunk routes well beyond the privatisation of London Buses. Eventually the need to meet accessibility regulations led to their removal, however, and the last examples finished on route 159 on 9 December 2005. Nevertheless, two heritage routes were started, shadowing parts of routes 9 and 15 with Routemaster operation. The routes ran daily between 09.30 and 18.30, and although aimed at tourists, normal fares and passes were accepted. A launch event was held on 14 November 2005.

First Group operated route 9 between Aldwych and the Royal Albert Hall. The Routemasters were refurbished and repainted to original-style livery, except for RM1650, which had been previously repainted into the 1977 Silver Jubilee livery as SRM3. It is seen in the Strand on 9 June 2006. The route was later altered to run from Trafalgar Square to Kensington High Street at the request of the Royal Borough of Kensington and Chelsea. When First Group sold their London operations in 2013, the route passed to Tower Transit. It ceased operating on 25 July 2014, following the introduction of LT class 'New Routemasters' on route 9.

Stagecoach work route 15. Typifying the superb condition to which the buses were prepared when the service started, RM324 is seen at Tower Hill on 19 November 2005. The route has continued into 2018, with the vehicles operating from Stratford garage.

Golden Tours

Golden Tours started competing on the sightseeing tour market on 18 June 2011, with tours departing from Buckingham Palace Road, Victoria. As of 2018 they offer a Blue Route Essential Tour with live English commentary, a Red Route Classic Tour and an Orange Route Grand Tour. There are morning and evening feeder services along Bayswater Road from Holland Park or Notting Hill. One-day or 24-hour tickets are available – the latter offers a free river cruise and walking tour. There is a hop-on, hop-off treasure hunt game and a London by Night open-top tour is also operated.

Golden Tours also operate an express service from Victoria, Baker Street and Kings Cross to the Warner Bros. film studios at Leavesden, near Watford, for studio tours of 'The Making of Harry Potter'. The service runs from April to December and Victoria/Baker Street departures are hourly. There is one morning departure from Paddington and one morning and one afternoon departure from King's Cross.

A newcomer on the sightseeing scene, Golden Tours started competing in 2011 with former Stagecoach London Alexander-bodied Dennis Tridents. V138 MEV stands in Buckingham Palace Road, Victoria, on 10 August 2011.

Golden Tours also operate an express service from Victoria to the Warner Bros. studio tour near Watford, where the *Harry Potter* films were made. Closed-top buses are used in overall *Harry Potter*-themed advertising (including contravision windows). One of them, Trident V168 MEV, is seen at Victoria on 14 April 2012.

There were also some new buses used, in the shape of three Volvo B9TLs with Optare Visionaire bodywork. You will have noted that bodies of a similar design were being supplied to Arriva TOLST and Big Bus at this time. On 18 June 2011, YJ11 OHO was in plain blue 'as delivered' condition.

Now fully kitted out, YJ11 OHN is on the Buckingham Palace Road stand on 6 August 2011.

More new buses followed in 2013, but this time they were Volvo B9TLs with MCV bodywork. 110 heads around Marble Arch on 20 July.

The ex-Stagecoach Tridents remained, and here 156 (V156 MEV) heads down Park Lane towards Hyde Park Corner on 9 March 2014.

Closed-top MCV-bodied Volvos were also bought for the *Harry Potter* tour. BF62 UYP has just entered Park Lane at Marble Arch on a return journey to Victoria on 6 April 2017.

More new MCV-bodied Volvos came in 2016, but these carry the EvoSeti style of bodywork, which was also entering service with Go-Ahead London for tendered bus work (in closed-top form of course!). 136 is also seen at Marble Arch on 2 July 2016.

London City Tour

London City Tour entered the fray on 23 March 2015, taking on Arriva TOLST, Big Bus and Golden Tours. They are owned by Spanish coach group Julià. They also operate City Tour services in a number of other cities worldwide, including Barcelona, Mexico City, Rome and San Francisco.

In 2018 they offered two hop-on, hop-off circular routes, the shorter Red Route and the longer Blue Route, which operate every ten to twenty minutes from 08.30 to 18.00. Tickets are valid for 24 or 48 hours and a recorded commentary is provided in ten languages. The customary river cruise and walking tour options are provided, there is a free voucher book, which gives discount vouchers for various attractions and restaurants, and free Wi-Fi and an app are also available.

London City Tour started with a batch of former Metroline Volvo B7TLs with Plaxton bodies. One of these vehicles passes the familiar location of St Paul's Cathedral in March 2015.

For the 2018 season the fleet was upgraded with some Volvo B9TLs with Wright bodywork. BF60 UUC still shows its former Metroline number, VW1846, although it was new to First London. Seating is now PO37/29F.

Harrods

In 2012 the name and livery of Harrods appeared again, this time on a pair of Routemasters. I found these rather elusive vehicles and managed this picture of RML2621 in Fleet Street on 18 August. I am not sure who was operating these on behalf of Harrods, though it was probably Premium Tours, as both Routemasters were working for them two years later. Premium Tours continue to offer a tour including cream tea at Harrods.

The other bus in Harrods livery was RM1979, seen passing St Paul's on the same day (18 August).

Premium Tours

A few other operators have joined in, providing less frequent, but more specialised tour options. Premium Tours of Chiswick offered a tour that includes the 'View from The Shard'. Opened in 2012, The Shard, next to London Bridge station, is the UK's tallest building. It includes a public viewing gallery, which has become a tourist attraction to rival the London Eye and the passengers (not the bus!) make their way up to the gallery as part of the tour. Another of their specialist tours is an evening 'Jack the Ripper' tour.

Traditional Routemasters have been sourced to work for Premium Tours, and former RM1979 is seen at Victoria on 21 June 2014. This was the vehicle seen in Harrods colours in 2012.

Another of Premium Tours' buses is RML2621, although this did not carry the full lettering when seen parked on the Embankment on 22 March 2015. It had also previously been running in Harrods livery in 2012.

Ghost Bus Tours/Classic Tour

A different approach to tourism is offered by Ghost Bus Tours Ltd. Trading as London Necrobus, they use Routemasters on their evening Ghost Bus Tours, which start from Northumberland Avenue and visit places not on the other company's routes. They also operate similar services in York and Edinburgh, again with Routemasters.

RML2516, seen on 24 September 2014 among traffic in the Strand by Charing Cross station, promises to take travellers to Trafalgar Scare, Notting Hell and Earls Corpse!

Two of their Routemasters – open-top RM1398 (KGJ 118A) and RM2203 (CUV 203C) – are operated as the Classic Tour and carry this patriotically adorned version of the LT red livery. RM1398 was seen in Whitehall on 27 December 2016.

Brigit's Afternoon Tea Bus Tours

This company offers a different approach in that their buses – all Routemasters – have been fitted with tables and patrons are served afternoon tea and cakes while enjoying their tour. Departures are from Northumberland Avenue and Victoria coach station. In April 2018 there were six RMs and four RMLs in the fleet. A single RM also runs tours in Bath (do they serve Bath buns?).

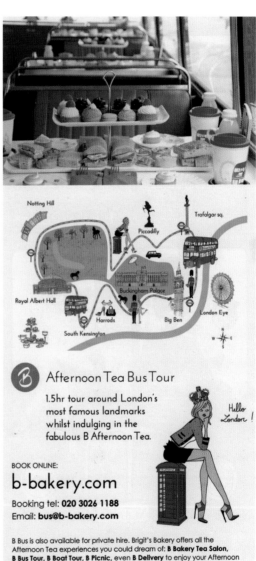

Showing that there is still room for the niche market provider, B Bakery has been very successful, offering Afternoon Tea Bus Tours. Utilising Routemasters (what else!) now fitted out with tables, patrons can enjoy a tour of London while indulging in a luxury afternoon tea. RM1735 is entering the top side of Marble Arch from Bayswater Road on 6 September 2018.

Stagecoach London – Megasightseeing

From March 2018 nine Stagecoach London Dennis Tridents in the 184** batch were converted to open-top (four full and five part open-top). The first conversion was 18475, named *King Henry VIII*, which became fully open-topped and blue with megasightseeing. com lettering. Sightseeing tours in London were due to begin on St George's Day, 23 April 2018. In practice they started before this; buses were running from Saturday 21st at least. An hourly, non-stopping service is planned between 10.00 and 17.00 from three boarding points, with extra services during the busy seasons. A taped English language commentary will be provided. Tours will need to be pre-booked online like the Megabus coach services. In a way, this almost mirrors the early days of the RLST, but with a modern twist in the booking method.

The first Stagecoach vehicle to be converted for their Megasightseeing service, 18475 *King Henry VIII*, was an entry at the South East Bus Festival at Detling Showground, near Maidstone, on 7 April 2018.

Will it succeed? Well, Megabus has grown substantially since it was introduced in August 2003 with the same marketing concept of pre-booked online seats from £1. In a press release, Paul Lynch, MD of Stagecoach London, said: 'We are so proud to be launching this new product. With our superb value tickets this is not only a fantastic service for tourists coming to London but for people living or working in or around London who might have a couple of hours to spare, or friends and relatives visiting from out of town. With our great value tickets a family can enjoy a day out for a great price.'

Representing the part open-top conversions, 18467 *King George V* heads up Park Lane on 15 May.

Postscript

At the end of 2017 there were four main companies providing sightseeing tours: RATP, trading as The Original London Sightseeing Tour (TOLST), Big Bus Company, Golden Tours, and London City Tour. The first two of these are established companies with modern fleets. Golden Tours are a relative newcomer but have carved out a role for themselves and invested heavily in new vehicles. London City Tour are also a newer company but have foreign backing. The 2018 season opened with a new competitor in Stagecoach with their Megasightseeing concept. Could all these companies survive? Well, in August 2018 it was announced that London City Tours were entering a partnership with RATP-TOLST. The London City Tour fleet was being reported as being advertised for sale, and by September a number of TOLST vehicles had been given City Tour colours.

Meanwhile, the heritage Routemaster operation may have been scaled down with the ending of route 9, but route 15 continues at present. Ghost Bus Tours and the growth of specialist operator B Bakery with their Afternoon Tea Bus Tour shows that there is still room for a niche company who can offer something a little different – and they use Routemasters! Moreover, a privately owned Routemaster has been successfully fitted with the latest Euro 6 emissions standard engine, so it shows that these iconic London buses so loved by tourists can still be adapted for a tourism role in the future.

Bibliography

Baker, Michael H. C., *London Transport From the 1930s to the 1950s* (Hersham: Ian Allen, 2009).

Baker, Michael H. C., *London Transport Since 1933* (Shepperton: Ian Allen, 2000).

Lane, Kevin, *London Half-Cab Farewell* (Hersham: Ian Allen, 2009).

Lloyd, Colin and Grimes, Keith, *London Bus Handbook: Part 2* (Harrow Weald: Capital Transport, 1993).

Wharmby, Matthew and Rixon, Geoff, *Routemaster Omnibus* (Hersham: Ian Allen, 2008).

Wilson, Tony, *'On the Tourist Trail in London'* (*London Bus Magazine*, summer 2006).

Buses monthly magazine from 1970 (Shepperton/Hersham: Ian Allen).

Various publications including fleet lists and newsletters by the London Omnibus Traction Society have also been referenced. This is the principal society for enthusiasts of London Transport and its successors, and anyone with an interest in the London bus scene is recommended to join. www.lots.org.uk

Websites and leaflets of the current sightseeing tour operators have also been invaluable sources.